The MAILBOX®

The Education Center

Organize MARCH Now!™

Everything You Need for a Successful March

Monthly Organizing Tools
Manage your time, classroom, and students with monthly organizational tools.

Essential Skills Practice
Practice essential skills this month with engaging activities and reproducibles.

March in the Classroom
Carry your monthly themes into every corner of the classroom.

Ready-to-Go Learning Centers and Skills Practice
Bring March to life right now!

D1470003

Managing Editor: Sharon Murphy

Editorial Team: Becky S. Andrews, Kimberley Bruck, Karen P. Shelton, Diane Badden, Thad H. McLaurin, Kimberly Brugger-Murphy, Cindy K. Daoust, Gerri Primak, Karen A. Brudnak, Hope Rodgers, Dorothy C. McKinney, Janet Boyce, Jennifer Brahos, Catherine Broome-Kehm, Rebecca Brudwick, Stacie Stone Davis, Margaret Elliott, Angie Kutzer, Beth Marquardt, Christy McNeal, Sheila Ransom, Susan Walker

Production Team: Lisa K. Pitts, Pam Crane, Rebecca Saunders, David G. Bullard, Jennifer Tipton Cappoen, Chris Curry, Sarah Foreman, Theresa Lewis Goode, Clint Moore, Greg D. Rieves, Barry Slate, Donna K. Teal, Zane Williard, Tazmen Carlisle, Cat Collins, Marsha Heim, Amy Kirtley-Hill, Lynette Dickerson, Mark Rainey, Angela Kamstra, Sheila Krill

www.themailbox.com

©2006 The Mailbox®
All rights reserved.
ISBN10 #1-56234-686-5 • ISBN13 #978-156234-686-7

Table of Contents

Monthly Organizing Tools

A collection of reproducible forms, notes, and other timesavers and organizational tools just for March.

Essential Skills Practice

Fun, skill-building activities and reproducibles that combine the skills your students must learn with favorite March themes.

March in the Classroom

In a hurry to find a specific type of March activity? It's right here!

Ready-to-Go Learning Centers and Skills Practice

Two center activities you can tear out and use almost instantly! Plus a collection of additional reproducible skill builders!

Skills Grid

	Spring	Wind	Rainbows	St. Patrick's Day	Centers	Games	Time Fillers	Writing Ideas & Prompts	Learning Center: A Timely Rainbow	Learning Center: High Flyers	Ready-to-Go Skills Practice
Literacy											
alphabetical order		30									
initial consonant: *l*	25										
ending sounds: *n, s, t*			40								
long-vowel word families: *-ail, -ake*											92
short and long vowels		29									
counting syllables										82, 89	
short and long vowel: *e*			41								
sort words by category	18										
color words			34			63					90
rhyming words						62					
compound words			36								
contractions					58						
sight words					59						
sight words or spelling words				44							
capitalization	19										
capitalization: places				48							
punctuation	26										
journal prompts								70			
writing	21	28	37	45				70			
sentence writing			35								
sequencing sentences											91
descriptive words					43						
descriptive writing								71			
skill review	20			42			69				
Math											
number identification						62					
number sequence						63	69				
ordinal numbers				44							
comparing sets					58						
addition to 16			36								
subtraction				45							
place value											96
fractions	20										
positional words				43							
shape combinations	18										
nonstandard measurement			37								
shorter and longer				49							
coin combinations to 50¢	27										
coin amounts											93
time to the hour										74, 81	94
time to the half hour		33								74, 81	
money					59						
graphing											95
probability	21										
patterns		28		42							
story problems	19	29									
skill review	20		34								
Science											
data collection		30									
understanding weather phenomena			35								

Medallion

Tape to a student's clothing or glue to a crepe paper necklace.

Brag Tag

Award

JUST BLOWIN' BY TO SAY

_____ _____
teacher   date

Medallion, brag tag, and award: Copy onto colorful construction paper, cut out, and use as desired.

March

Sunday	Monday	Tuesday	Wednesday	Thursday	Friday	Saturday

Center Checklist

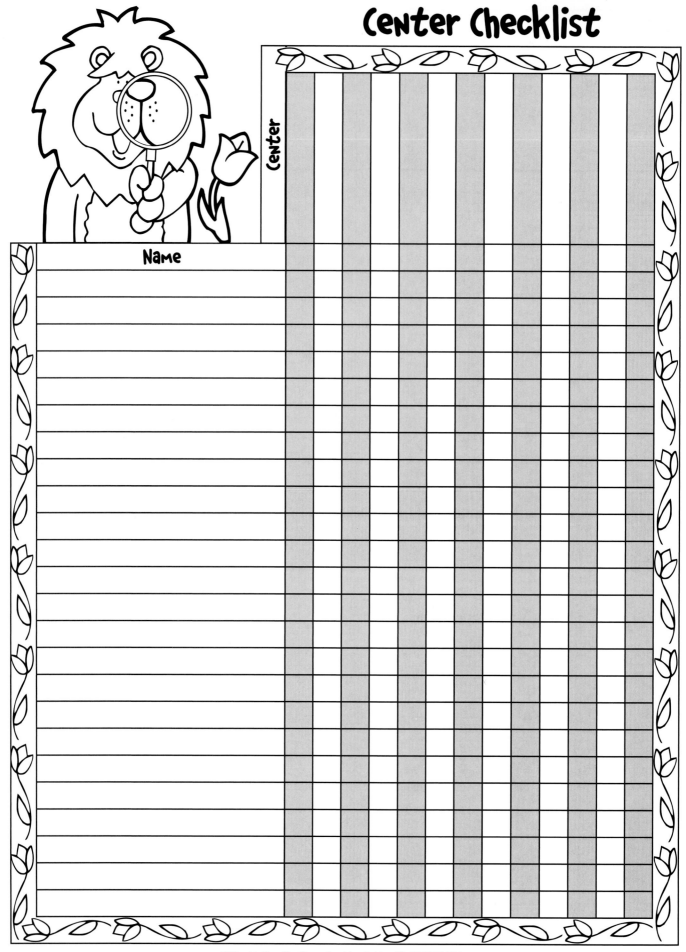

Center

Name

Class List

Name											

Classroom News

From _____

Date _____

Help Wanted

Special Thanks

Look What We Are Learning

Please Remember

Superstars

Classroom News

From _____

Date _____

©The Mailbox® • *Organize March Now!*™ • TEC60981

Clip art: Use the artwork on student papers and on correspondence such as announcements, forms, and parent notes.

Name _____

Goal _____

You're soaring!

©The Mailbox® • *Organize March Now!*™ • TEC60981

Keep trying!

Name _____

Goal _____

©The Mailbox® • *Organize March Now!*™ • TEC60981

Name _____

Goal _____

Go for it!

©The Mailbox® • *Organize March Now!*™ • TEC60981

Incentive charts: Have students track their progress as they work toward a variety of goals.

My Journal

Name _____

Journal cover: Make this page the front cover of your students' writing journals.

Materials to Collect:

Duties This Month:

Meetings:

Birthdays & Special Dates:

Themes:

To Do:

Monthly planning form: Use this handy form to stay on top of March's school-related responsibilities.

Open: Use this page for parent correspondence, or use it with students too. For example, ask each child to write (or dictate as you write) a story about two friends, Leo the lion and Lacy the lamb; have her write word problems starring these two critters; or have her list words or draw pictures of words that begin with *l*.

Dear Parent,

Please remember

_____
date

Thanks!

Parent reminder note: Use this note to remind parents of supply requests, field trips, and special events such as a classroom party, a school program, or a guest speaker.

SCHOOL NOTE

SCHOOL NOTE

School notes: Use these notes for parent communications such as announcing an upcoming event, requesting supplies or volunteers, and writing messages of praise.

This colorful quilt block will contribute to a rainbow display in your child's classroom. Have your child look through old magazines for pictures that are the same color as the block. (If magazines are not available, have him or her draw pictures of objects that are this color.) After cutting out the pictures or drawings, have your child glue them to the block.

We hope to see your completed project by _____.

Sincerely,

Name _____

Learning Links: fine-motor skills, colors

Note to the teacher: Date and sign a copy of the page. Make student copies on construction paper in assorted rainbow colors. When a child returns her project and shares it with the class, arrange the blocks in a quilt design. Add the title "Our Cozy Rainbow Colors."

Spring

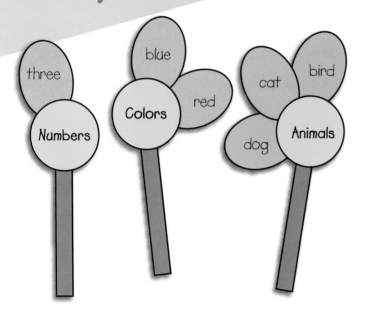

Build a Flower

To prepare for this center, cut out three construction paper circles and a supply of construction paper petals. Glue a paper stem to each circle to resemble a flower without petals. Label each flower with a different category, such as colors, numbers, or animals. For each category, program several petals each with a different word. Place the petals and flowers at a center. When a child visits the center, she selects a petal, reads the word, and places it around the appropriate flower. She continues in this manner until all the petals have been placed.

Kite Puzzler

Youngsters' geometry skills soar to new heights with this thought-provoking puzzle! Give each child a white construction paper kite cutout, divided into sections similar to the one shown. Have him color the kite and cut along the lines to form smaller shapes. Instruct each student to mix his shapes and combine them to make different designs. Encourage youngsters to share their creations with classmates who are sitting nearby. For an added challenge, have each student arrange his shapes to form the original kite. (Post a completed kite to serve as a model.) Then have him glue his kite to a large sheet of construction paper and incorporate the kite into a picture.

Birds chirping, flowers blooming, and breezy days are sure signs that spring is on its way! Welcome the season with this sunny skill-based unit!

Story problems • • • • • • • • • • • • Math

Duck Tales

Obtain several small rubber ducks for use with this splashy small-group activity. Place the ducks on a large pond cutout and gather a group of students around the pond. Say a story problem that involves ducks and a pond. Then invite a student to solve the problem using the ducks as manipulatives. Once students are comfortable with the activity, invite a volunteer to create a story problem and have the other youngsters solve it. If desired, place the ducks and pond at a center so partners may practice creating and solving story problems.

Two ducks are splashing in the pond. One more duck dives in. How many ducks are playing in the pond?

Literacy • • • • • • • • • • • • • • • • Capitalization

Wild or Woolly?

Name Ilyssa

Thursday, March 1, 2007
Friday, March 2, 2007
Monday, March 5, 2007

Tuesday, March 6, 2007

There were _____ days. There were _____ days.

Wild and Woolly Weather

The coming of spring brings about unpredictable weather; some days are fierce like a lion and some are calm like a lamb. Use this class activity to keep track of March weather while reviewing capitalization of days and months. Give each child a copy of the recording sheet on page 22. Have her write her name and color the pictures. Each day in March, enlist students' help in deciding whether the weather is more like a lion or a lamb. Then write the full date on the board, omitting all capitalization. Direct each youngster to rewrite the date using proper capitalization in the corresponding column of her recording sheet. At the end of the month, ask each child to count the days in each column and complete the sentences at the bottom of her sheet.

Glorious Gardens

When youngsters work together to draw these gardens, their understanding of fractional parts is sure to grow! To prepare three gardens, divide one sheet of bulletin board paper into halves, one into thirds, and one into fourths. Divide students into three groups and give each group a different garden.

To begin, have each group draw a different type of vegetable in each garden section. Then help youngsters label each section with its fractional part. Post the completed gardens in a prominent location. Have volunteers use fractions to describe a chosen garden. For example, a child could say that one-third of the garden has carrots. If desired, keep the gardens posted as a handy fraction reference.

Skill review

Literacy & Math

Fantastic Flowers

This versatile center is blooming with sorting skills! To prepare, glue a supply of construction paper flowers to green-painted craft sticks (stems). Then place a mound of play dough in each of two small plastic flowerpots. Program the flowers and pots for a grade-appropriate sorting skill, such as sorting addition facts by sums, odd and even numbers, initial consonants, word families, or contractions. Place the flowers and pots at a center. When a child visits the center, she sorts the flowers into the appropriate pots by pushing the stems into the play dough.

Spring Into Writing

With all of the changes that come along with the arrival of spring, it's no wonder youngsters' senses are aroused! Compile student-generated lists of things they can see, hear, smell, touch, and taste during spring. Help each child use the lists to complete a copy of the poem on page 23. Then have him color and cut out the poem. Mount each student's completed paper on a slightly larger sheet of construction paper. Display the poems on a board titled "Spring Has Sprung!"

Springtime Senses

Spring is here!

I see __sunshine__.

I smell __flowers__.

I hear __bees buzzing__.

I feel __warm air__.

I taste __strawberries__.

Spring is here!

by __Evan__

Which Animal?

To prepare for this small-group game, color and cut out a copy of the baby animal cards on page 24. Then cover a tissue box cube with construction paper and attach each card to a different side of the cube to resemble a large die. After a review of probability concepts, give each child in the group a copy of the recording sheet on page 24. Have a child roll the die and identify the baby animal that is faceup. Direct her to mark a tally in the appropriate row. After continuing in this manner for a predetermined number of rolls, have each child count the tallies in each row and write the corresponding number where indicated. Then invite youngsters to share their results.

Name __Miriam__

Which Animal?

Find reproducible activities on pages 25–27.

Wild or Woolly?

Name _____

There were _____  days.   There were _____ days.

Note to the teacher: Use with "Wild and Woolly Weather" on page 19.

Springtime Senses

Spring is here!

I see _____.

I smell _____.

I hear _____.

I feel _____.

I taste _____.

Spring is here!

by _____

TEC60981

Baby Animal Picture Cards

Use with "Which Animal?" on page 21.

Name _____

Which Animal?

	Total	Total	Total	Total	Total	Total

Note to the teacher: Use with "Which Animal?" on page 21.

Lemonade Break!

Name _____

✂ Cut. 🧴 Glue the pictures that begin with **l**.

Fragrant Flowers

Name _____

✏️ Write a . or a ? in each box.

🖍️ Color the petals as you go.

Skunk smells the flowers ☐

Does he think the flowers smell good ☐

He thinks the flowers smell bad ☐

Skunk thinks he smells good ☐

Do you think Skunk is right ☐

Skunk goes to the garden ☐

The flowers are pretty ☐

Will Skunk pick some flowers ☐

What kind of flowers will he pick ☐

He picks two daisies ☐

Shopping for Seeds

Name _____

✏ Write the amount.

Find the seed packet that costs the same.

Circle the seed name on the chart.

Beans	Lettuce	Carrots	Peppers	Peas	Radishes
36¢	21¢	50¢	45¢	32¢	42¢

Seeds for Sale!

A.	_____ ¢	peppers radishes
B.	_____ ¢	lettuce beans
C.	_____ ¢	peas radishes
D.	_____ ¢	carrots lettuce
E.	_____ ¢	carrots beans
F.	_____ ¢	peas peppers

Wind

Math • • • • • • • • • • • • • • • • • Patterns

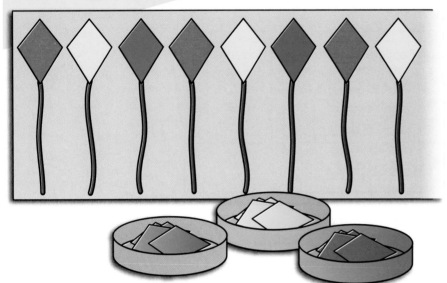

Kites in a Row

Place a length of blue bulletin board paper at a center. Draw a row of kite strings on the paper as shown. Make a supply of construction paper kite cutouts in three different colors. Then sort the kites into separate containers and place them at the center. A child places a kite at the top of each string to make a pattern. He reads the pattern and removes the kites. Then he repeats the process to make different patterns.

Writing • • • • • • • • • • • • • • Literacy

A Blustery Book

Read aloud the book *The Wind Blew* by Pat Hutchins. Give each child a 9" x 12" sheet of construction paper. Invite her to write about something the wind blew and where it blew the object. Then have her draw a picture to match. Stack the pages and bind them to the right-hand side of a 12" x 18" sheet of tagboard to make a class book. Color and cut out a copy of the wind character on page 31; then glue it to the left-hand side of the book. Add the title shown. After reading the finished book to your youngsters, place it in your reading center for students to look at independently.

What did the wind blow?

The wind blew my bicycle, and it landed in a tree.

Look what the March winds blew in—a seasonal collection of skill-based ideas just right for your students!

Wonderful Windsocks

Spotlight long vowels and short vowels with these fun and functional windsocks! Give each child a 9" x 12" sheet of construction paper, six crepe paper streamers, and a copy of page 32. Have half of the students label their papers "Long Vowels" and the remaining students label their papers "Short Vowels." Then help each student roll her paper into a cylinder and staple it in place. Have each child cut out her picture cards. Then instruct her to find the cards with pictures whose names represent her vowel sound. Have her color the chosen cards and glue each one to the end of a different length of streamer. Direct her to glue the remaining end of each streamer to the bottom of the cylinder. After the glue dries, add yarn hangers to the resulting windsocks.

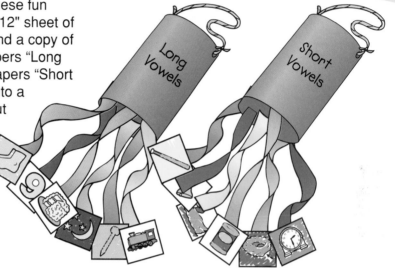

Laundry on the Line

Who knew that unruly laundry could be the source of oodles of entertaining story problems! Gather a supply of T-shirts or T-shirt cutouts. Place the shirts in a basket with a supply of spring-style clothespins. Suspend string between two chairs to resemble a clothesline. To begin, attach five shirts to the clothesline. Explain that five shirts were drying on the line when the wind began to blow very hard. Prompt youngsters to pretend to be the wind and say, "Whoosh, whoosh, whoosh!" Then have a volunteer remove some of the shirts from the line and drop them to the floor as if the wind blew them down. Help a student write the corresponding subtraction problem and solution on your board. Continue in the same way, changing the numbers used for each story problem.

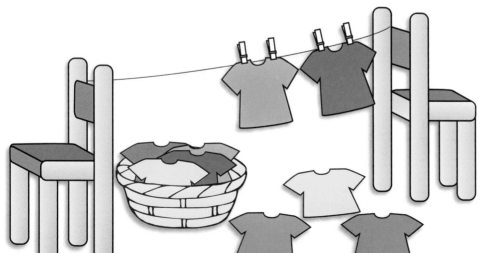

Objects	Will it move?	Did it move?
⬤	No	Yes
◇	Yes	Yes
✂	No	Yes
📎	Yes	Yes

Name _Lee_

Does It Move?
Listen for directions.

Blowin' in the Wind

Youngsters predict and then test whether the wind will cause a variety of objects to move. Give each child a copy of the recording sheet on page 31, a straw, and each of the following items: a cotton ball, a piece of paper, a pair of scissors, and a jumbo paper clip. He writes his name on the paper. He predicts which items will move when blown with air and which items will not; then he writes his predictions in the second column on his sheet. Next, he tests each prediction by pointing his straw at an object and blowing a steady stream of air through the straw. He writes the results of each test in the final column.

Alphabetical order

Literacy

Mixed-Up Letters

Attach alphabet cards to your board in a random arrangement. Then explain to students that a strong breeze has blown the cards around so that they are no longer in the correct arrangement. Have a youngster find the letter *a* card and place it at the far left-hand side of the board. Continue in the same way with each remaining letter in sequential order. For a more advanced version, have students order cards that you've labeled with wind-related words.

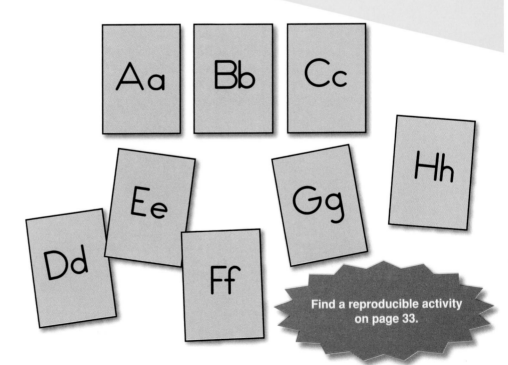

Find a reproducible activity on page 33.

TEC60981

Does It Move?

Name _____

Listen for directions.

Objects	Will it move?	Did it move?

Note to the teacher: Use with "Blowin' in the Wind" on page 30.

Picture Cards

Use with "Wonderful Windsocks" on page 29.

©The Mailbox® • *Organize March Now!*™ • TEC60981

Time Flies!

Name _____

✏️ Write each time.

Time to the Half Hour **33**

Rainbows

Sort by odd and even.

A Rainbow Review

To prepare for this center, color and cut out a copy of the rainbow pattern on page 53. Also make a supply of cloud cutouts to fit on either end of the rainbow. Program the clouds for sorting. Consider skills such as odd and even numbers, numbers greater than or less than 50, and correct or incorrect answers. Code the backs of the cutouts for self-checking. A child visiting this center sorts the clouds onto opposite ends of the rainbow.

Super Streamers

Write on separate large index cards each of the following color words: *red, orange, yellow, green, blue,* and *purple.* Also write the word *rainbow* on each of two separate index cards. Then mix all of the cards. To begin, give each youngster a length of crepe paper streamer, making sure that each color is represented by at least one student. Show students a color word card; then encourage the children with the corresponding color of streamers to stand up and say the name of the color as they wave their streamers in the air. Continue in the same way with each remaining card. When a rainbow card is revealed, encourage all of the students to stand up and say the word *rainbow* as they wave their streamers!

purple

Youngsters are sure to treasure this colorful
collection of rainbow-themed ideas!

Vivid Sentences

With this rainbow packed full of words,
youngsters can make a variety of giggle-
inducing sentences! Draw a rainbow
on a sheet of paper. Then label each
color with the words shown. Display
the rainbow near a table stocked with
markers and strips of paper. To make
a sentence, a child chooses one word
from each color, working from the top
of the rainbow to the bottom. He writes
his completed sentence on the provided
paper. Display students' work around the
rainbow.

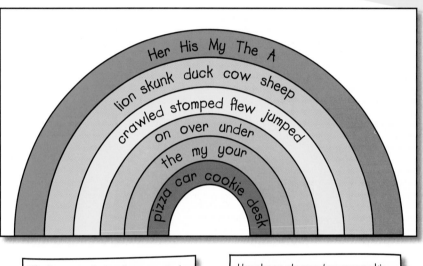

Her His My The A
lion skunk duck cow sheep
crawled stomped flew jumped
on over under
the my your
pizza car cookie desk

The lion crawled under your desk.

Her sheep stomped on my cookie.

His skunk jumped on my pizza.

Pop-Up Rainbow

Help students understand why rainbows occur with a project that's sure to
be "pop-ular"! For each child, make a copy of the project strips on page 38
and the rainbow on page 39. To begin, give each youngster a 9" x 12" sheet
of light blue construction paper, folded in half. Encourage each child to cut out
her project strips and glue them to the front
of the folded paper as shown. Then have
her draw a sun, a cloud, and raindrops. Next,
have her color and cut out her rainbow
pattern. Encourage each child to fold her
rainbow in half and fold the tabs back. Then
help her tape the rainbow to the inside of
the project so that the tabs are in a slanted
position as shown. Have each youngster
refold her project. Then read aloud the project
as youngsters follow along.

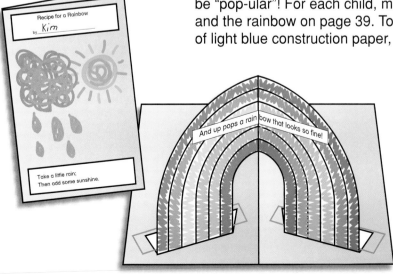

Recipe for a Rainbow
by Kim

Take a little rain;
Then add some sunshine.

And up pops a rainbow that looks so fine!

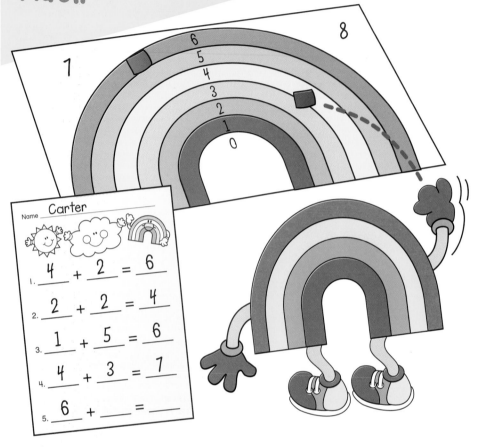

Toss It!

Draw a rainbow on a sheet of bulletin board paper; then label the paper with different numbers as shown. Place the paper on the floor. Provide access to two beanbags and a class supply of the recording sheet at the bottom of page 38. A child writes his name on a sheet. Then he tosses the beanbags on the rainbow paper and writes the two numbers on his sheet to make an addition problem. He solves the problem and writes his answer in the blank. Then he collects the beanbags and repeats the process for each remaining space on the sheet.

Compound words

Rain + Bow = Rainbow!

No doubt you'll hear giggles aplenty with this nifty whole-group idea! Write a variety of compound words on sentence strips. Then cut the words apart and place the resulting cards in random order face-down in a pocket chart. Explain that the word *rainbow* is made up of two separate words: *rain* and *bow.* Next, have a student turn over two cards. Help the student read the resulting compound word. If it is a real compound word, have the student place the cards together. If it is not a real compound word, have her flip the cards back over. Continue playing in the same way, similar to the game of Memory, until all the cards have been paired correctly.

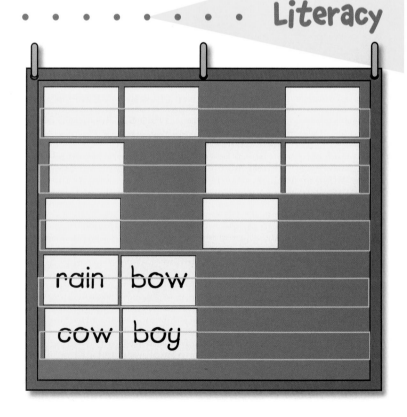

• • • • • • • • • • • • • • •

A Rainbow of Words
by Juliana

truck   hair
stop sign   fire
strawberry

A Brilliant Booklet

Give each child a set of construction paper booklet strips in rainbow colors. Have each youngster stack the pages in rainbow order. Then staple the pages between two cloud cutouts to make a booklet. Direct each child to title the booklet as shown. Then instruct her to write on each page of her booklet the name of at least one object of that color. When their booklets are finished, have students take them home to share with their families.

Math • • • • • • • • • • • • • • • *Nonstandard measurement*

Colorful Craft Sticks

When students visit this center, they measure clouds with a rainbow of craft sticks! Make four white cloud cutouts in different sizes, making sure that a specific number of craft sticks can be placed end to end along the length of each cloud. Draw a straight line, as shown, across the length of each cloud. Then place the clouds at a center along with a supply of colored craft sticks. A student visits the center and lays craft sticks along the line on a cloud. Then he counts the craft sticks used to measure the cloud. He continues in the same way for each remaining cloud.

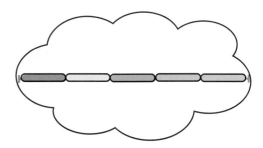

Find reproducible activities on pages 40–41.

Recipe for a Rainbow

by_____

Take a little rain;
Then add some sunshine.

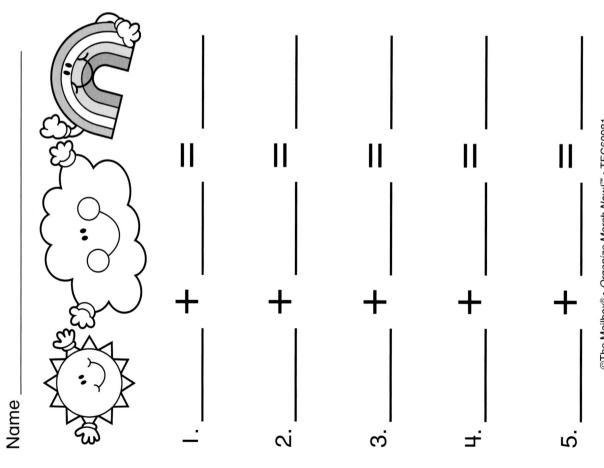

Name _____

1. ___ + ___ = ___

2. ___ + ___ = ___

3. ___ + ___ = ___

4. ___ + ___ = ___

5. ___ + ___ = ___

©The Mailbox® • *Organize March Now!*™ • TEC60981

Note to the teacher: Use with "Toss It!" on page 36.

Use with “Pop-Up Rainbow” on page 35.

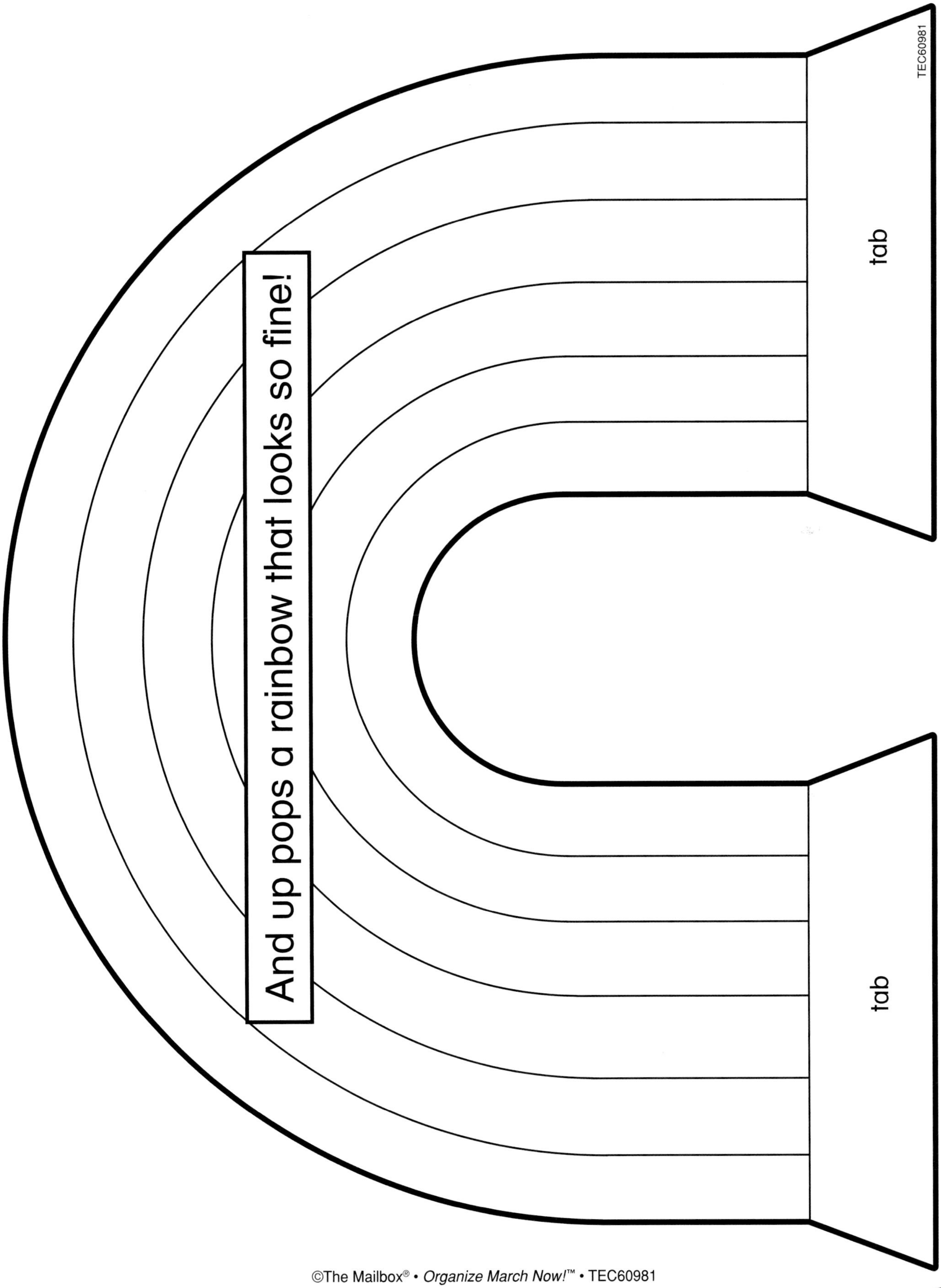

TEC60981
tab
And up pops a rainbow that looks so fine!
tab

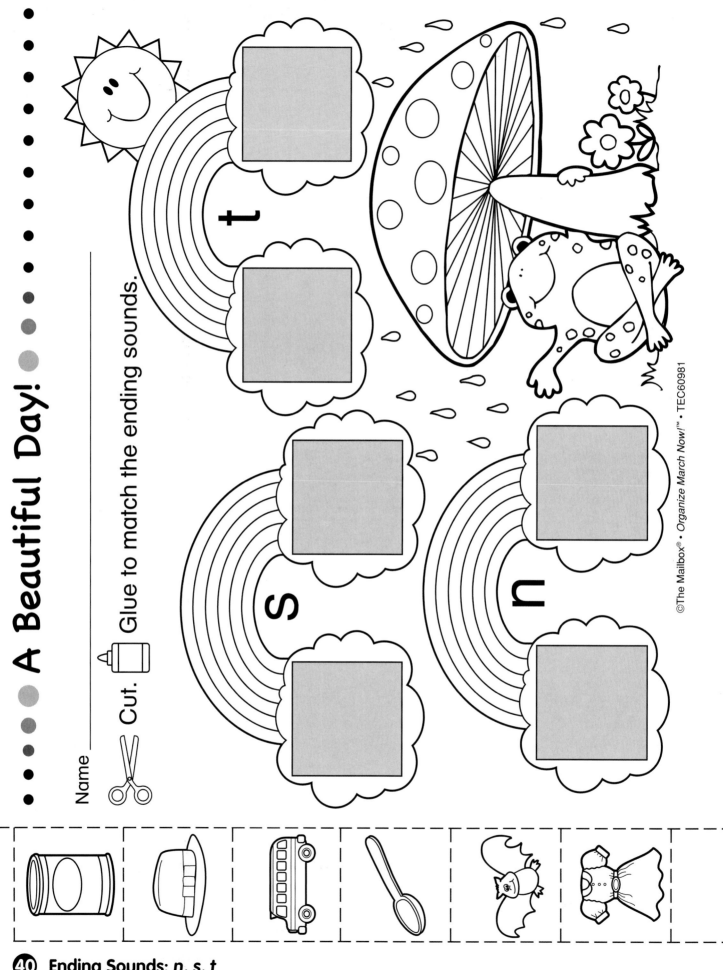

A Beautiful Day!

Name _____

Cut. Glue to match the ending sounds.

t

s

n

40 Ending Sounds: n, s, t

What a Sight!

Name _____

✏️ Write the words to match the vowel sounds.

Use the word bank.

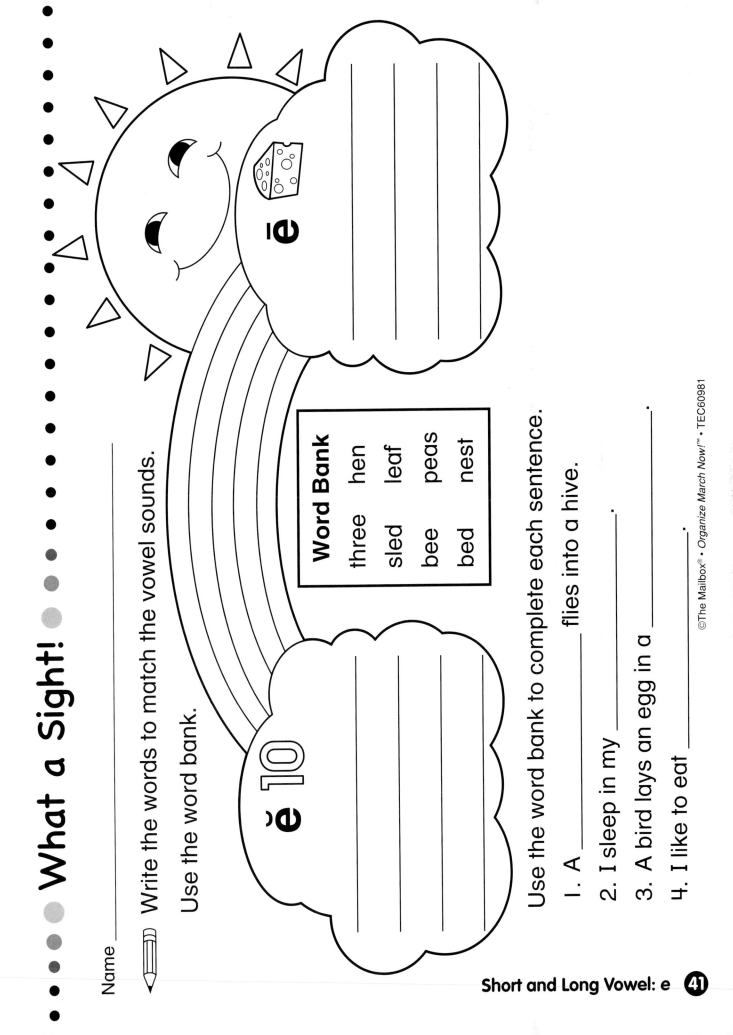

ē

ĕ 10

Word Bank

three	hen	leaf
sled	bee	peas
bed	nest	

Use the word bank to complete each sentence.

1. A _____ flies into a hive.

2. I sleep in my _____.

3. A bird lays an egg in a _____.

4. I like to eat _____.

St. Patrick's Day

• *Skill review*

A Field of Shamrocks

Use the patterns on page 64 to make a supply of green tagboard shamrocks. Cut out the shapes and label half of the cutouts with a grade-appropriate skill, such as contractions, vowel sounds, or beginning letters. Then program the other half to correspond. Before children arrive for the day, scatter the shamrocks on the floor in your large-group area. For added fun, scatter gold confetti around the shamrocks. To begin, explain to the students that a mysterious field of shamrocks has sprouted in the classroom. Next, have a child "pick" two shamrocks and identify whether they correspond to each other. If they do, have her place the cutouts in a pocket chart. If they do not, have her return them to the floor. Continue in the same way with additional volunteers.

Patterns • *Math*

Little Green Shoes

No doubt fashionable leprechauns have little green shoes in several styles. That makes their shoes perfect for patterning practice! Make several green construction paper copies of the shoe patterns on page 46. Store each style of shoes in a separate shoebox at a center. Invite two youngsters to visit the center. Each child makes a pattern for his partner to identify and extend.

Sprinkle this selection of St. Patrick's Day activities throughout the month of March. They're worth their weight in gold!

Positional words • • • • • • •

Where Could It Be?

Youngsters describe the location of a leprechaun's bar of gold with this whole-group activity! Wrap a rectangular block with yellow cellophane or construction paper to resemble a bar of gold. Gather students in a circle and hand the gold bar to a child. Ask him to pretend to be a leprechaun and hide the gold while his classmates close their eyes. Upon his return to the circle, ask the child to use a sentence with a positional word to announce where the gold is. As a volunteer tracks down the gold, use the format shown to begin a list of students' hiding spots for later reading practice. Repeat the activity until each child has had a turn to hide or retrieve the gold.

> **Searching for Gold**
> Tanya hid the gold <u>under</u> her desk.
> Jamal hid the gold <u>behind</u> the beanbag.
> Sam hid the gold <u>in</u> the sink.

Math

Literacy • • • • • • • • • • • • Descriptive words

Make It Sparkle!

Make a supply of large yellow coin cutouts. On sentence strips write the sentence shown, omitting the words on the coins. Then cut the sentence apart. To begin, read aloud the sentence as you place each word in a pocket chart. Explain that the sentence is fine the way it is, but with the addition of a few extra words it could be much more exciting. Ask a youngster to share a word that might describe a leprechaun. Write the word on a coin cutout and place it in the appropriate location on the chart. Continue in the same way, having students share words to describe the gold, the patch, and the shamrocks. Then read the final sentence.

For more advanced students, write descriptive words on coin cutouts and place them at a center. Challenge a student to choose three coins and use the words in a sentence to describe a leprechaun.

The (happy) leprechaun counted his (shiny) gold in a (huge) patch of (green) shamrocks.

Literacy

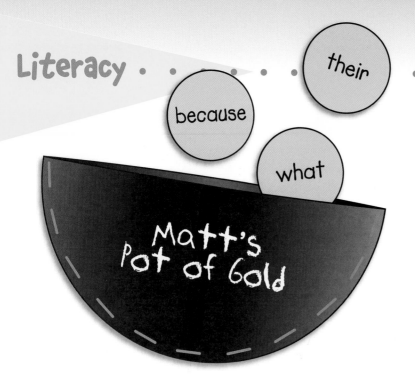

because · their · what

Matt's Pot of Gold

Words to Remember

For each child, staple two semicircles of black construction paper together to resemble a black pot. Have each child use a white crayon to personalize a pot. Then give him several gold coin cutouts. Have him write a sight word or spelling word on each gold coin and place it in his pot. Instruct youngsters to use the coins to quiz each other on the words, or have them take the pots home each day to review the words with a family member.

Ordinal numbers

Math

Five Dancing Leprechauns

Recite the rhyme below to your youngsters. Then give each child a copy of page 47. Begin reciting the rhyme again, stopping after the description of the first leprechaun. Encourage each child to locate the first leprechaun on his sheet and use an orange crayon to draw a wig. Continue in the same way with each remaining leprechaun, having each student add any embellishments as mentioned in the rhyme. When the youngsters are finished, ask them questions about the leprechauns' positions, such as "Which leprechaun is holding a bunch of flowers?" It's the fourth one!

Five little leprechauns danced a jig.

The first one wore a big orange wig.

The second one carried a pot of gold.

The third one picked a shamrock to hold.

The fourth one had a bunch of flowers.

The fifth one said, "I could dance for hours!"

So the five little leprechauns danced away

On that lovely St. Patrick's Day!

Five Dancing Leprechauns

Name _____

Listen for directions.

I could dance for hours!

Pots of Gold

To prepare for this partner game, write a different subtraction problem on each of 20 blank cards. Give each youngster a black pot cutout and a small cup of ten round crackers to resemble gold pieces. To play, the twosome stacks the cards facedown between them. In turn, each player turns over a card from the stack and states the answer. The student with the larger difference places a cracker on his pot. Then the partners place their cards to the side and repeat the activity. The pair continues in this manner until one child places all ten of his gold pieces on his pot. Then invite the youngsters to munch on their gold!

$$\begin{array}{r} 12 \\ -\ 6 \\ \hline \end{array}$$

$$\begin{array}{r} 14 \\ -\ 9 \\ \hline \end{array}$$

What's in the Leprechaun's Pot?

by Ms. Tou's class

Andrea

The leprechaun has a pot of dirty socks. It smells very bad. He should wash them.

No Gold Here!

What other items might a leprechaun put in his pot instead of gold? Your youngsters are sure to have a few creative ideas! Have each child glue a black pot cutout to the center of a 9" x 12" sheet of construction paper. Then explain that a leprechaun had a pot full of gold, but he gave all of the gold away and now all he has is a pot. Ask students what the leprechaun might put in his empty pot. Have each student draw her chosen item or items in her pot; then have her write about her drawing. Stack all of the completed papers. Bind them together with a cover titled as shown. Finally, read aloud the finished class book to your youngsters.

Find reproducible activities on pages 48–49.

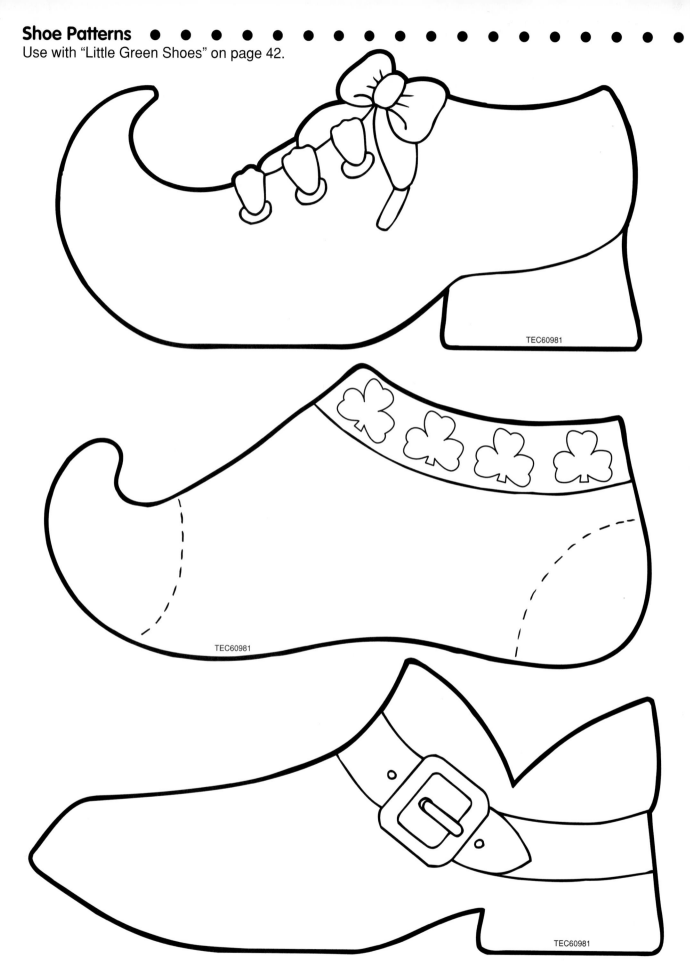

TEC60981

TEC60981

TEC60981

©The Mailbox® • *Organize March Now!*™ • TEC60981

Five Dancing Leprechauns

Name _____

Listen for directions.

Note to the teacher: Use with "Five Dancing Leprechauns" on page 44.

A Terrific Trip

Name _____

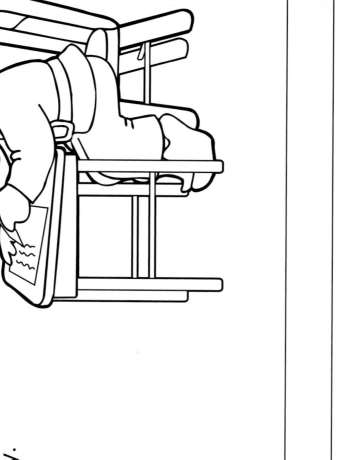

✏️ Circle the name of each place that is missing a capital letter.

✏️ Write the name of each place correctly.

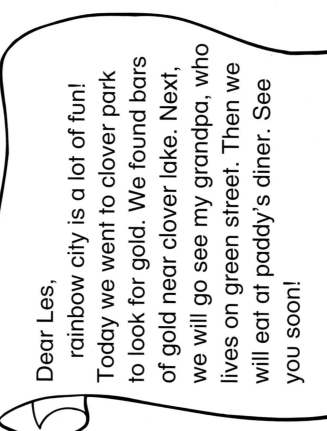

Dear Les,

rainbow city is a lot of fun! Today we went to clover park to look for gold. We found bars of gold near clover lake. Next, we will go see my grandpa, who lives on green street. Then we will eat at paddy's diner. See you soon!

Your friend,
Lucky

1. _____

2. _____

3. _____

4. _____

5. _____

Capitalization: Places

Leprechaun Lengths

Name _____

🖍 Color the object that is longer.

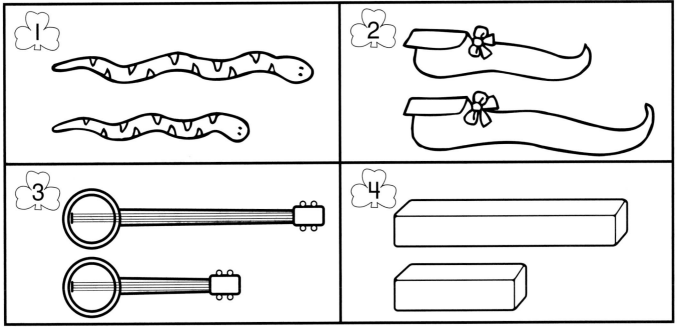

🖍 Color the object that is shorter.

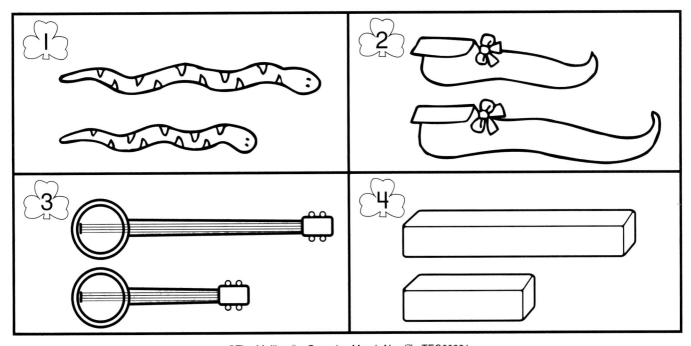

Arts & Crafts

Step 2

Lion or Lamb

Welcome the month of March with this wild and woolly two-sided project!

Materials for one project:
small cardboard tube
2½" x 6" yellow construction paper strip
four 4" bamboo sticks or twigs
yellow construction paper lion head (pattern on page 52)
white construction paper lamb head (pattern on page 52)
small orange tissue paper strips
cotton balls
glue
sharpened pencil

Steps:
1. Cover half of the tube with the yellow paper.
2. Use the pencil to poke four leg holes in the tube as shown.
3. Push one end of each stick into a different hole and seal with glue. Allow time for the glue to dry.
4. Glue tissue paper around the lion head to resemble a mane and then glue the lion head to the yellow end of the tube.
5. Glue cotton balls to the other half of the tube to resemble lamb's wool.
6. Glue the lamb head to the free end of the tube.

Rainbow Blending

Use colored chalk to color every other arc of a construction paper copy of the rainbow pattern on page 53 as shown. Then use a spray bottle to spray the rainbow with a light mist of water. With one finger, gently rub together the two colors on each side of each blank arc. The primary colors will blend together, forming a different color in each blank arc. After the rainbow is dry, cut it out and glue it to a sheet of light blue construction paper. Then add cotton ball clouds.

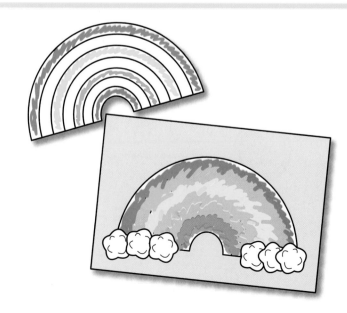

Shamrock Search

Cut a large shamrock from a 12" x 18" sheet of white construction paper. Use a variety of green objects and paint to make several small shamrocks and one four-leaf clover on the large shamrock. Consider using the following green objects: O-shaped cereal pieces, colored reinforcement rings, craft foam, tissue paper, or sticky dots. Then draw green stems on the shamrocks and the four-leaf clover. Mount the large shamrock to a slightly larger sheet of green construction paper and trim it to make a border. Have students trade shamrocks with their classmates and search for four-leaf clovers!

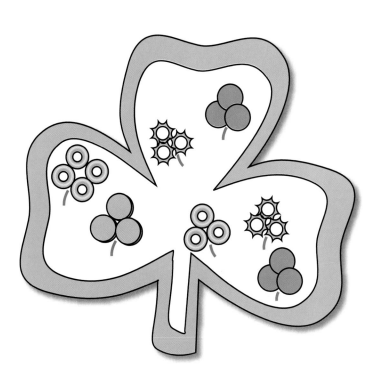

Spring Songbird

Place the straight edge of a tagboard bird cutout (pattern on page 52) along the crease of a folded sheet of construction paper. Trace the bird and then cut it out, leaving the fold intact. Use markers to decorate both sides of the folded bird. Then fold down the wings and decorate the blank sides. Unfold the bird, squeeze glue along one of the undecorated sides of its body (not on the wings), and add a ribbon hanger. Then refold the bird to secure the two sides together. If desired, glue craft feathers to the bird's wings and body.

Lion and Lamb Patterns
Use with "Lion or Lamb" on page 50.

TEC60981

TEC60981

Bird Pattern
Use with "Spring Songbird" on page 51.

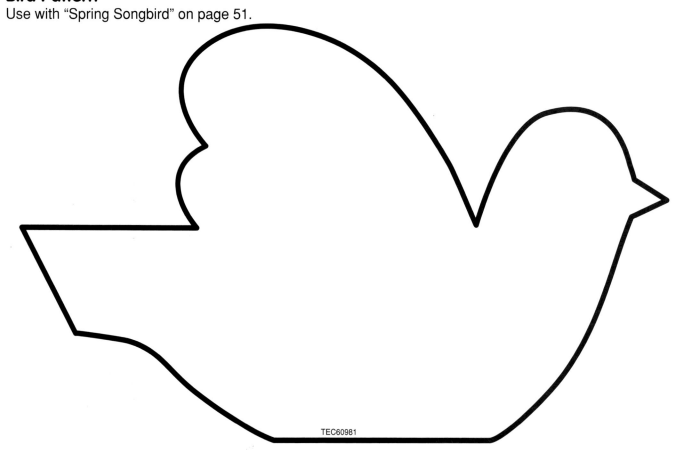

TEC60981

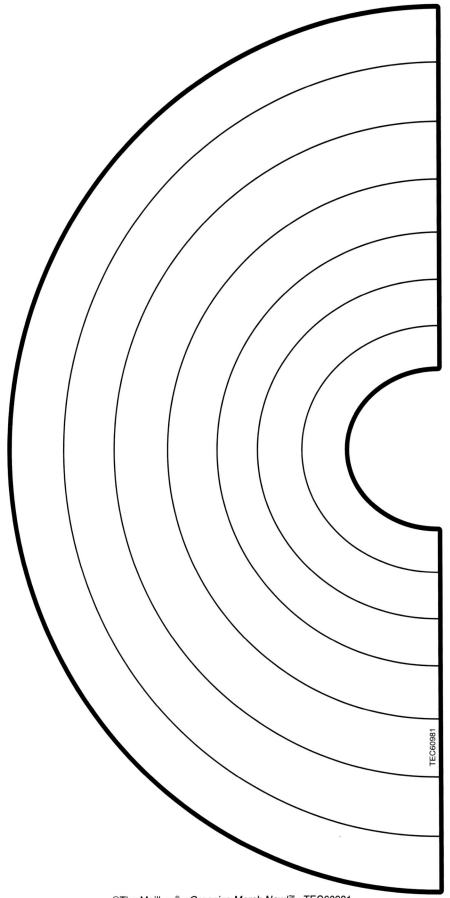

TEC60981

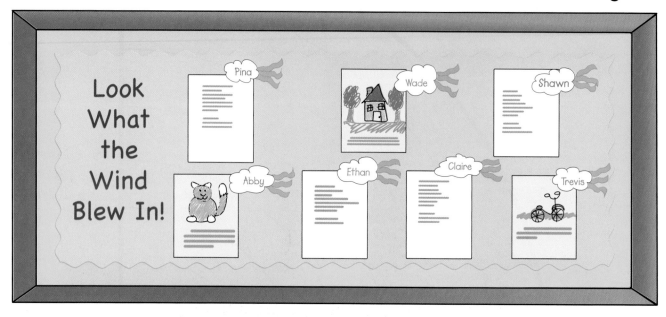

Look What the Wind Blew In!

Have each child cut out a cloud shape from a 4" x 6" piece of white construction paper. Then direct him to curl three four-inch light blue construction paper strips by wrapping each strip around a pencil and then unwrapping it. After he personalizes the cloud, have him glue the strips to the cloud to resemble blowing wind. Ask each child to choose a sample of his best work; then display each work sample with its corresponding cloud and the title shown.

To prepare, cut a bell pepper in half and remove the seeds. Have each student make a green pepper print on the left side of a nine-inch construction paper strip to resemble a four-leaf clover; then set the strip aside to dry. On a sheet of paper, ask each child to write and draw about a time when she was lucky. Direct her to label the paper strip with the title "My Lucky Day" and then glue it to the top of her paper. Display the completed projects along with the title shown.

Displays

Enlarge the leprechaun pattern on page 56; then color it and cut it out. Display the leprechaun next to a large black paper pot titled "We're Golden!" Have each child glue a provided picture of himself to a gold construction paper coin. After he decorates his coin with glitter, mount each coin to the pot as shown.

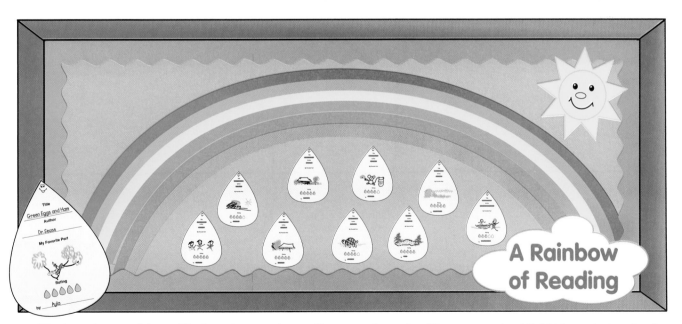

Display a large rainbow, titled as shown, along with a sun character. Place a supply of light blue raindrop book reports (pattern on page 57) near the display. After a child reads a book independently or with a parent's help, she completes a form as indicated. Then she rates the book on a scale from one to five, with five as the best rating, by coloring in the desired amount of small raindrops. Mount the completed reports on the board.

Leprechaun Pattern

Use with "We're Golden!" on page 55.

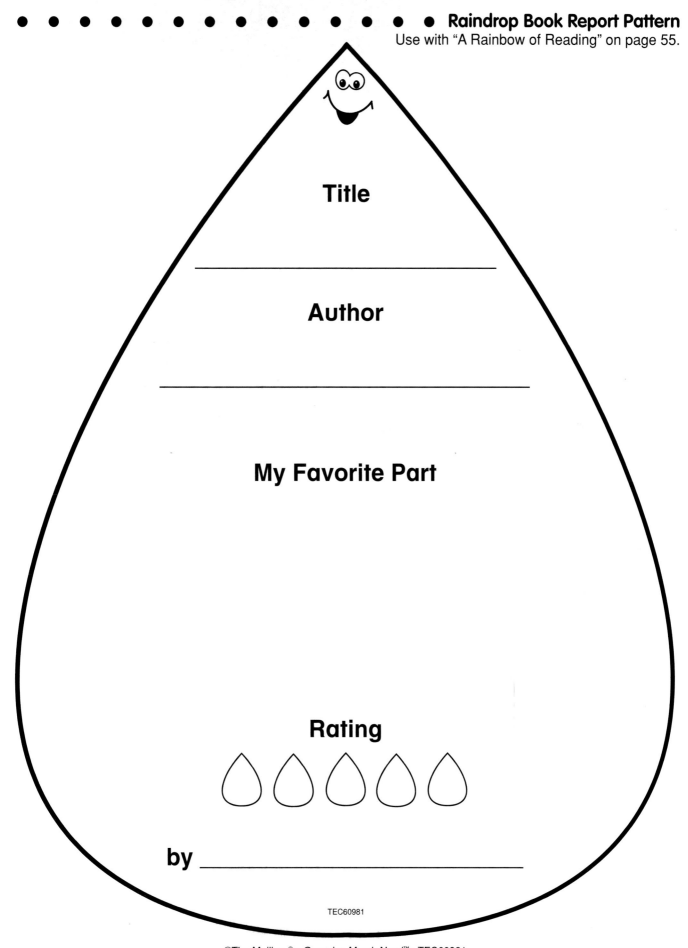

Title

_____

Author

_____

My Favorite Part

Rating

by _____

TEC60981

Centers

Literacy

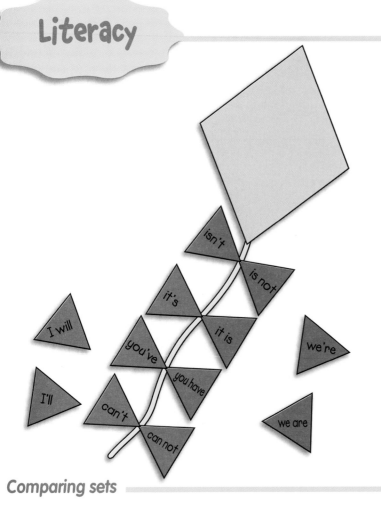

Up, Up, and Away!

Make a kite cutout and several pairs of triangle cutouts. Tape the kite to a flat surface; then attach a yarn tail. Label one triangle in each pair with a contraction and each corresponding triangle with the two words used to make the contraction. Place the triangles near the kite. A student visits the center and chooses a triangle labeled with a contraction. He finds the corresponding triangle and places them on opposite sides of the kite string to resemble a bow. He continues in the same way with each remaining pair of triangles.

Comparing sets

Math

Lions and Lambs

For this partner center, make a yellow construction paper copy of the lion pattern on page 60 and a white construction paper copy of the lamb pattern on page 61. Cut out the patterns and place them at a center with a large die and a supply of yellow and white pom-poms. Two youngsters visit the center and each child takes a cutout. One student rolls the die and places the corresponding number of matching pom-poms on her cutout. Her partner repeats the process; then the children decide who has more pom-poms and who has fewer pom-poms. After a decision is made, they remove the pom-poms from their cutouts and play another round!

Seeds for Sale

Gather five seed packets and place them in a small plastic flowerpot. (If the prices marked on the packets are too challenging for your students, mark them out with a permanent marker and reprice the packets according to student ability.) Place the container at a center along with a supply of play money. A child chooses a packet from a container. Then she counts out the coins needed to purchase the packet. She continues in the same way with each remaining seed packet.

Gathering Gold

Youngsters identify sight words and help a little leprechaun collect his scattered pieces of gold! Place at a center a black plastic container or pot. Write a sight word on each of several yellow tagboard circles (gold). Scatter the gold around the pot. To begin, explain to students that the leprechaun has spilled his pot of gold and needs your students' help to pick it up. Then invite two youngsters to the center. The students take turns picking up a piece of gold, identifying the sight word, and then placing it in the pot. When all the gold is back in the pot, the children dump it out again for the next pair of student visitors.

Lion Pattern

Use with "Lions and Lambs" on page 58.

TEC60981

TEC60981

Games

Literacy

Rhyming words

The Cat's Hats

In honor of Dr. Seuss's birthday, March 2, have youngsters supply these well-known hats with their missing stripes! From bulletin board paper, cut two large red hats similar to the hat worn by Dr. Seuss's character the Cat in the Hat. Write "cat" on one hat and "red" on the other. Also make several white paper strips sized to fit the hats as shown. Label half of the strips with different words that rhyme with the word *cat.* Label the remaining strips with words that rhyme with the word *red.* Store the strips in a bag and lay the hats on the floor in different areas of the classroom.

To play, seat students in a circle. As you pass the bag around the circle, have each child take a strip and silently identify whether the word rhymes with *cat* or *red.* On your signal, have students walk to the corresponding hat. In turn, have each child read his word and place it on the hat. Then collect the strips and play the game again.

sat
bat
hat
cat

shed
bed
sled
fed
red

led

mat

rat

sped

Number identification

Math

The Leprechaun Shuffle

Youngsters pretend to be leprechauns in this whole-group activity. To prepare, make a class supply of yellow coin cutouts. Label each coin with a different number. Have youngsters stand in a circle; then give each student a coin cutout and have her place it on the floor in front of her. Play a recording of music, such as Irish folk music, and have students walk around the circle. Stop the music and then instruct each child to stop in front of a coin and pick it up. Go around the circle, having each youngster identify the number on her cutout. Then have her place it back on the floor for another round!

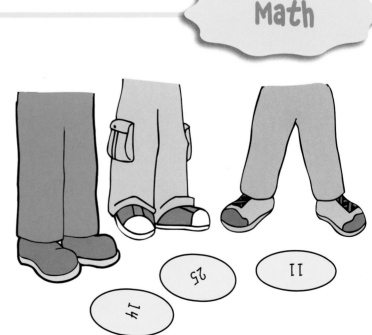

25

11

14

Math

Shamrock Lineup

Tailor this game to reinforce any range of numbers. Cut out a supply of green construction paper copies of the shamrock patterns on page 64. Number the cutouts with a chosen sequence of numbers; then mix them up and place them in a bag. To begin, invite students, in turn, to choose a shamrock and set it on the board ledge to arrange the numbers in a row from least to greatest. Students take turns until the sequence is complete. For a more advanced version, number the shamrocks by twos, fives, or tens for skip-counting practice.

Literacy

Color word identification

Upset the Rainbow!

This color word activity gets little ones up and moving! Make a class supply of the color word cards on page 65, making sure there are at least two copies of each color word. Seat students in a circle. Then invite a child to sit in the center of the circle. Encourage him to say either the name of a color or "Upset the rainbow!" If he names a color, each youngster with the corresponding card stands up and switches places with another child holding a matching card. Each youngster must find a new spot if the child calls "Upset the rainbow!" Continue in the same way for several rounds. Then invite a new youngster to sit in the middle of the circle!

Shamrock Patterns ● ● ● ● ● ● ● ● ● ● ● ● ● ●

Use with "A Field of Shamrocks" on page 42 and "Shamrock Lineup" on page 63.

red

TEC60981

orange

TEC60981

yellow

TEC60981

green

TEC60981

blue

TEC60981

purple

TEC60981

Management Tips

A Golden Motivator

Use this class incentive idea to promote positive behavior. Post a large black paper pot on a board or wall. Copy the coin patterns on page 67 onto construction paper to make a supply; then cut them out and store them near the display. Each time youngsters exhibit a desired behavior, attach a coin to the pot. When the class earns a predetermined number of coins, reward youngsters with a small treat, a privilege, or copies of the award on page 67. This idea can also be used to motivate youngsters to complete homework, reinforce good attendance, or reward good work habits.

Groups in a Snap!

Ensure quick and random grouping of your youngsters with this simple idea! Label a class supply of seasonal cutouts, such as rainbows, shamrocks, or gold coins, each with a different student name. Then place the cutouts in a container. When an activity requires groups, simply draw the desired number of cutouts from the container to form each group.

Fresh as Spring

Looking for an easy way to display students' finest work? Create a clothesline display that's just in time for warm spring breezes! Secure a length of string beneath your chalkboard ledge and place a container of clothespins nearby. Clip a sample of each child's work to the line. To keep the display fresh, encourage students to routinely replace their work.

Time Fillers

Off With the Wind

When you're faced with a few extra minutes, ask each youngster to think about a place that he would like to go if the wind could carry him anywhere. Lead the class in the rhyme shown. Then have a volunteer name a chosen destination. Repeat the rhyme and then ask a different child to name a desired location. Continue in this manner as time allows.

Wind, oh wind, blow me away
To this place where I'd like to stay!

Thinking in Threes

The three leaflets of a shamrock are the inspiration for this creative-thinking idea. When you have a few unplanned moments, draw a shamrock on the board and count the leaflets with the class. Then invite youngsters to name different items that come in threes, such as wheels on a tricycle, sides of a triangle, colors on the United States flag, or lights on a traffic signal.

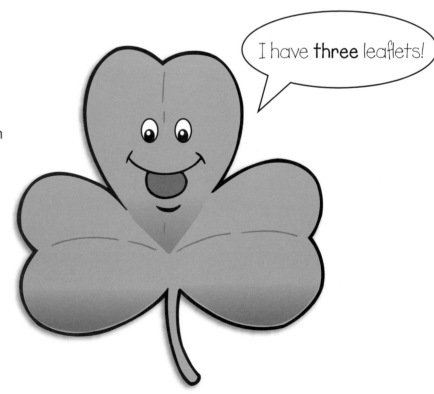

I have **three** leaflets!

Pot o' Review

Spark quick review sessions with a pot of gold! On each of several yellow construction paper circles (coins), write a different skill or concept that youngsters have already learned. Place the coins in a plastic cauldron-type pot or a box decorated to resemble a cauldron. Whenever you have a few extra minutes, invite a youngster to remove a coin from the pot. Then briefly review the related skill.

Addition facts to 12

Counting by tens

Words that begin with *ch*

31	32	33	34	🫕	36	37
41	42	☘	44	45	46	47
51	52	53	54	55	56	57
61	◆	63	64	🌈	66	67
71	72	73	74	75	76	77

Hidden Numbers

Use spare minutes to reinforce number order. Secretly cover a few numbers on your hundred chart each with a different small seasonal cutout or sticky note. Invite a volunteer to tell what number is behind a chosen cutout. Then remove the cutout to check her answer. Once all of the numbers have been revealed, have students close their eyes as you replace the cutouts in different positions on the chart.

Writing Ideas &

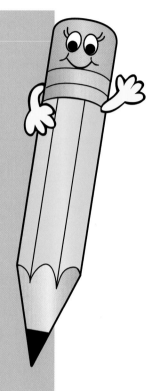

Journal Prompts

- Dr. Seuss was born on March 2, 1904. His real name was Theodor Seuss Geisel. Why do you think an author would choose not to use his or her ordinary name?

- Write a silly story about a day when the wind blew very hard.

- The first day of spring is in March. What do you like about spring?

- Pretend that you have picked a four-leaf clover and it brought you a day full of good luck. What would happen on such a day?

- Imagine being the same size as a leprechaun. Describe your day.

- What is the best way to catch a leprechaun?

- What would you do with your very own pot of gold?

Use one or more of the following ideas and the pot of gold pattern on page 72 to provide a golden writing experience for your youngsters!

Troy

The leprechaun let me have some gold. It was shiny. I took it home. Then I got a toy.

- Tell students that a leprechaun has led them to his pot of gold. Then have each child write about what might happen next on a copy of the pattern. When students are finished writing, encourage them to color the pattern, having them take care to color lightly over their writing. Then instruct them to spread glue on the gold coins and sprinkle glitter over the glue.

- Use the pot of gold pattern for journal writing. Copy the last journal prompt from above onto a copy of the pattern and add writing lines if desired. Then make a class supply.

- Give each child a copy of the pattern. Have each youngster pretend she is a leprechaun and write about the best place to hide her pot of gold.

Prompts

Sounds Tasty!

Commemorate National Nutrition Month with this fun descriptive-writing activity! Show youngsters samples of take-out menus, pointing out specific descriptive words that tempt the reader, such as *sweet, smooth,* and *juicy.* Write the words on a sheet of chart paper and encourage youngsters to share additional descriptive words. Next, give each child a circle cutout (plate). Have each youngster write and then describe a few of her favorite foods, using the words on the chart paper as a guide if needed. When she is finished, have her glue her plate to a 9" x 12" sheet of construction paper along with a plastic fork and napkin. Display the finished projects on a bulletin board.

Pizza: a tasty crust with spicy pepperoni

Ice cream: sweet chocolate ice cream with yummy cherries

Cookies: crunchy cookies with giant chocolate chips

There's a Mocket in My Pocket!

A mocket is green. It has purple hair and pink teeth.

Pocket Protectors

In honor of Dr. Seuss's March 2 birthday, read aloud his classic story *There's a Wocket in My Pocket!* Then point out that the words *wocket* and *pocket* rhyme. Have each child write the book title on a copy of the pocket cutout on page 73, replacing the word *wocket* with a different rhyming word. Have him color and cut out his pocket. Then have him glue it to a sheet of 9" x 12" construction paper, leaving the top portion of the cutout open to resemble a real pocket. Next, instruct each child to create his imaginary creature using scraps of construction paper. Have him tuck the creature in the pocket. Then have him write a description of the creature below the pocket.

TEC60981

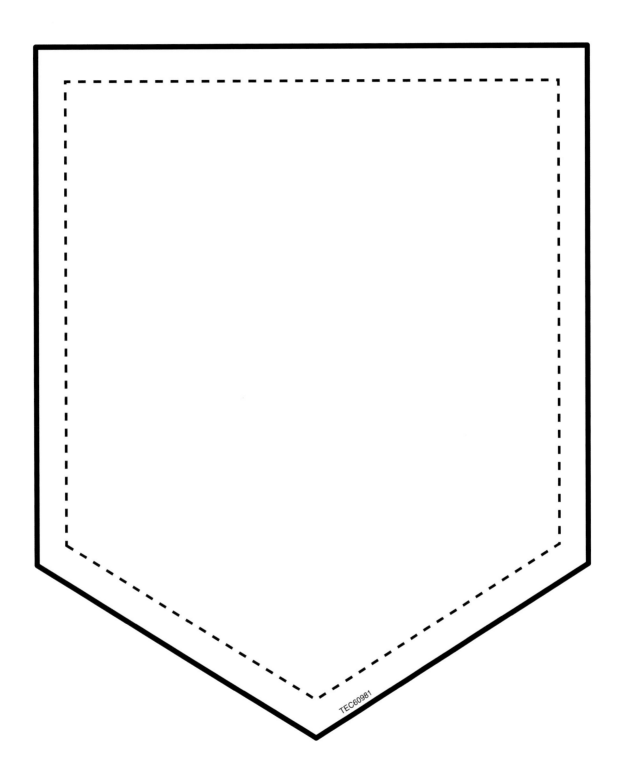

TEC60981

A Timely Rainbow

A ready-to-use center mat and cards for two different learning levels

Materials:

center mat to the right
center cards on page 77 (time to the hour)
center cards on page 79 (time to the half hour)
2 resealable plastic bags

Preparing the center:

Cut out the cards and select ones to make the best skill review for your youngsters. Store the remaining cards for later use.

Using the center:

1. A child removes the cards from a bag and lays them faceup in the center area.
2. He chooses a clock card and places it on a box on the mat. He finds the card that shows the matching digital time and places it on the remaining box.
3. To check his work, he turns over both cards. If the colored dots or triangles on the backs of the cards match, his work is complete. If they do not, he continues his work until he makes a match. Then he places both cards back in the bag.
4. He repeats Steps 2 and 3 for each remaining clock card.

Follow-Up

After a child completes the center activity for time to the hour and half hour, use the skill sheet on page 81 for more practice.

Clocks and Clouds

Name _____

✎ Write each time.

____ : ____

____ : ____

____ : ____

____ : ____

____ : ____

____ : ____

____ : ____

____ : ____

____ : ____

Time to the Hour and Half Hour 81

High Flyers

A ready-to-use center mat and cards

• • Counting syllables • • •

Materials:

center mat to the right
center cards on pages 85 and 87
resealable plastic bag

Preparing the center:

Cut out the cards and place them in the bag.

Using the center:

1. A child removes the cards from the bag and lays them faceup in the center area.
2. She chooses a card, says the name of the picture, and counts the number of syllables.
3. She places the card on the corresponding kite.
4. She repeats Steps 2 and 3 for each card.
5. To check her work, she flips over the cards on each kite. If the backs of the cards match, her work is complete. If they do not match, she recounts the syllables for the cards that are placed incorrectly and then places the cards on the correct kites.

High Flyers

Name the picture.
Count the word parts.
Put.

1   2   3

Follow-Up

After a child completes the center, use the skill sheet on page 89 for more practice.

Good Buddies!

Name _____

✂ Cut. 🖐 Count the word parts.

🧴 Glue.

1 1 2 2 3 3

Counting Syllables **89**

Name _____

✏️ Write to finish each color word.

🖍️ Color each kite to match the word.

blue
brown   red
orange   yellow
green   black

r _ _ _

b _ u _   gr _ _ _ _ _

bl _ _ _   y _ _ _ _ _ w

or _ _ g _   br _ _ _ _

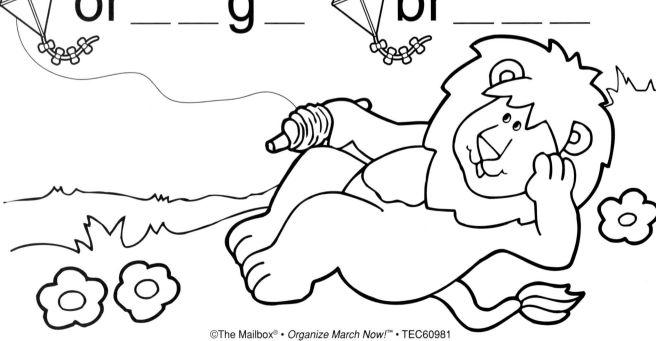

Looking for Gold

Name _____

Read. 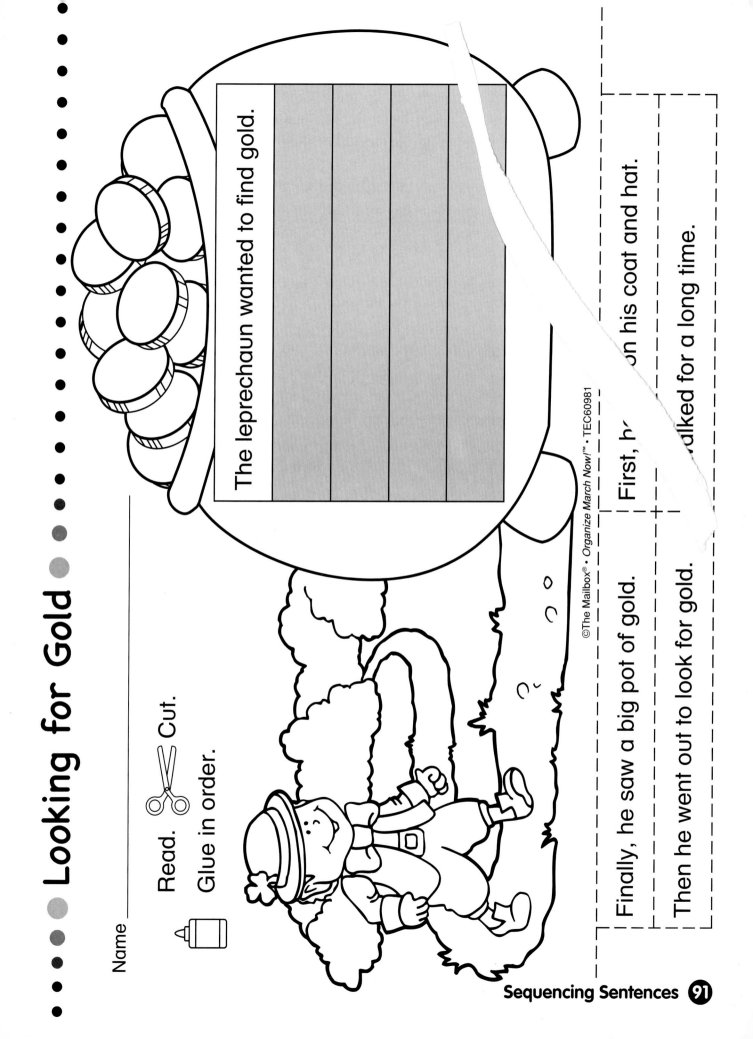 Cut.

Glue in order.

The leprechaun wanted to find gold.

First, h_ _n his coat and hat.

_alked for a long time.

Finally, he saw a big pot of gold.

Then he went out to look for gold.

Sequencing Sentences **91**

Brushing Up!

Name _____

✏ Write **-ail** or **-ake**.

✂ Cut.   Glue to match.

sn ___	sn ___
___ t	___ l
p ___	r ___
n ___	c ___
-ail	**-ake**

Long-Vowel Word Families: -ail, -ake

92

Welcome, Spring!

Name _____

✂ Cut. Match.

🗴 Glue.

1¢	
5¢	
10¢	

1¢	
5¢	
10¢	

Name _____

Color the box that shows the correct time.

The time is...

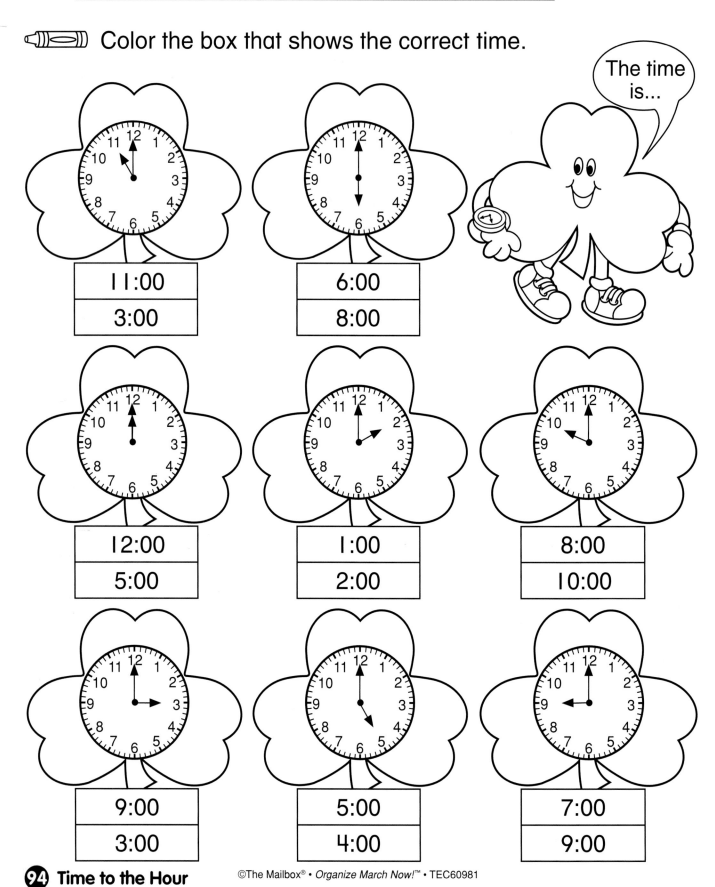

11:00
3:00

6:00
8:00

12:00
5:00

1:00
2:00

8:00
10:00

9:00
3:00

5:00
4:00

7:00
9:00

Cool Kites

Name _____

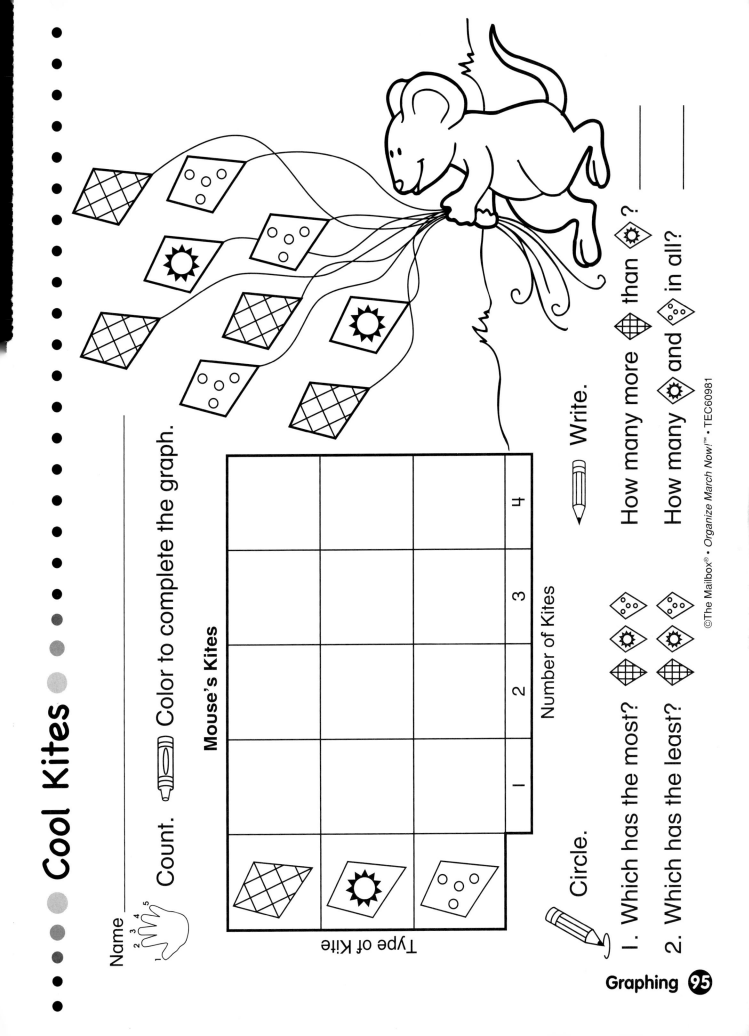

🖍 Count. Color to complete the graph.

Mouse's Kites

Type of Kite	1	2	3	4
(diamond pattern)				
(sun)				
(dots)				

Number of Kites

✏️ Write.

How many more ◈ than ✦ ? ____

How many ✦ and ∷ in all? ____

✏️ Circle.

1. Which has the most?   ◈ ✦ ∷

2. Which has the least?   ◈ ✦ ∷

Irish Stew

Name _____

Color the tens and ones by the code.

Write each number on the line.

Color Code
tens—green
ones—orange

3 tens 5 ones _____

6 tens 0 ones _____

8 tens 4 ones _____

7 tens 1 one _____

Place Value